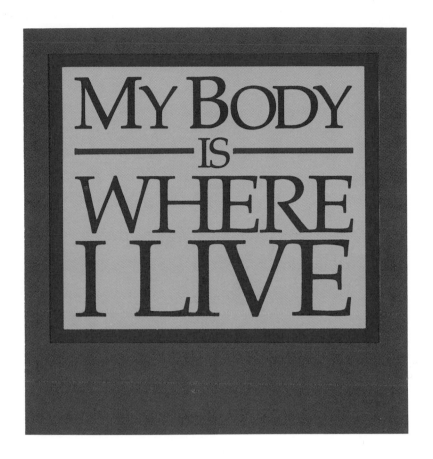

by Dorothy Baustian Chapman
Illustrated by Anastasia Mitchell

AGS ®
American Guidance Service
Circle Pines, Minnesota 55014-1796

This book was created to help children develop an appreciation of their body and an understanding of the dangers of drugs. *My Body Is Where I Live* is used with *Drug Free--A DUSO Approach to Preventing Drug Abuse.*

Design by Julie Nauman
Illustrations by Anastasia Mitchell

Printed in the United States of America

Library of Congress Catalog Card Number 88-083318
ISBN 0-88671-297-1
A 10 9 8 7 6 5 4 3

Dedicated to the memory
of my father
Rudolph A. Baustian
who, for 93 years, was
an exemplary caretaker of his body
DBC

My body is where I live,
the place where I think, feel,
learn, and grow.

From the safety of my body,
I reach out to the
smells, sounds, sights, and touch
of the world around me.

My body shows people how I feel.
Sometimes it sparkles with laughter...
cries out in pain...
rages with anger...
or trembles in fear.

My body is just
the right size for me.
When I grow,
it grows right along with me.

Sometimes I notice the bodies
of others...
different sizes, different shapes,
and different colors.

Sometimes I even think,
"I wish I had a body like that."

But then I look in the mirror
and say to myself,
"No, I like this one.
It's just right for me!"

My body is made of ordinary things
put together in a wonderful way
that is specially me!

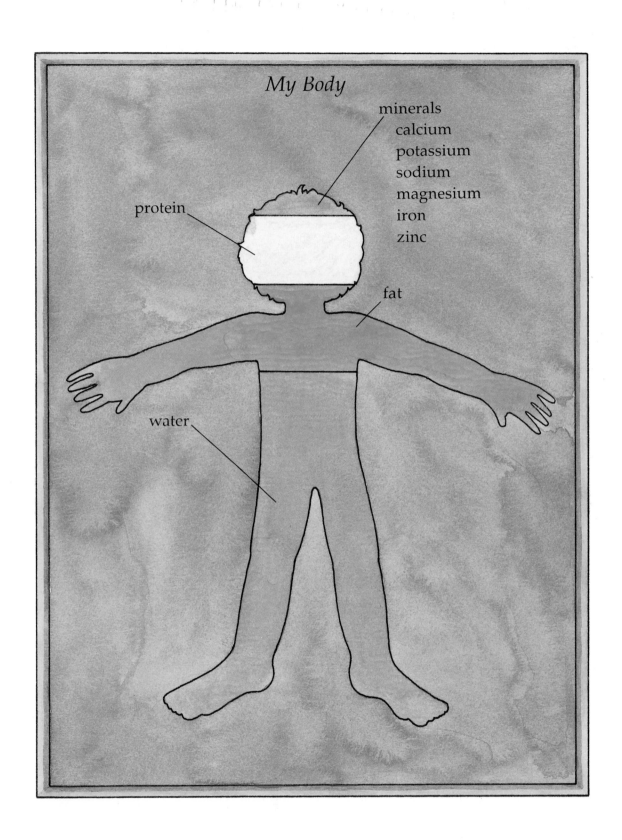

It's my job to take
care of my body,
to see that it gets what it needs
to stay healthy:
    food...
    exercise...
    rest...
    and water...inside *and* out...

What My Body Needs

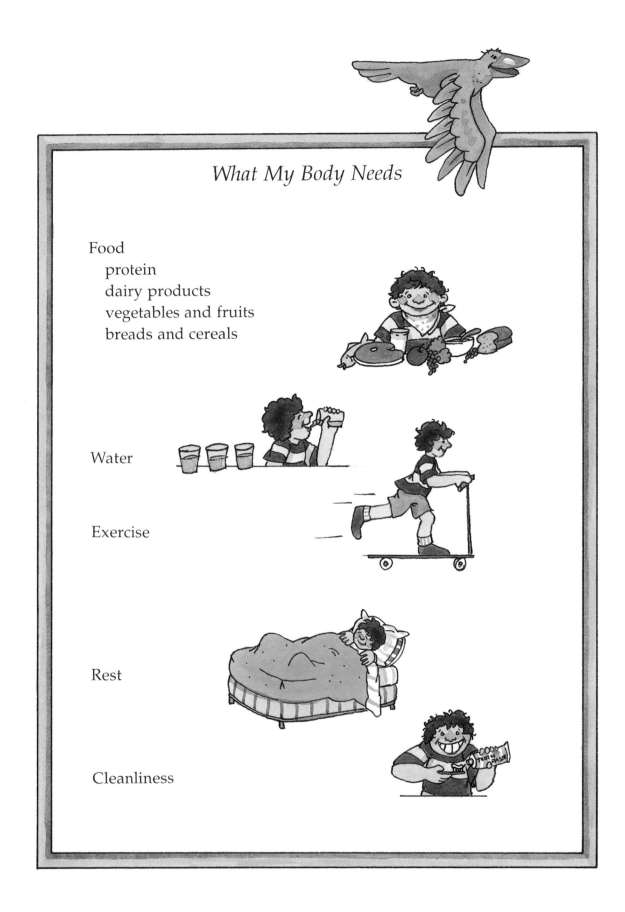

Food
 protein
 dairy products
 vegetables and fruits
 breads and cereals

Water

Exercise

Rest

Cleanliness

Once in a while something happens—
an accident, or an illness—
and I need to call in experts,
like a doctor, or a dentist,
and they take care of me.

Sometimes they give me medicine.
Not too much, not too little.
Just the right amount to help my body
start working again like a fine machine.

Then I try my best
to keep it that way...

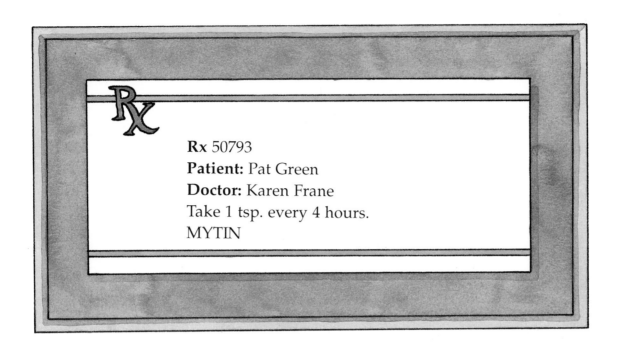

Rx 50793
Patient: Pat Green
Doctor: Karen Frane
Take 1 tsp. every 4 hours.
MYTIN

To do that, I need to know
how certain things affect the body.
Things like
   tobacco,
   alcohol,
   and other drugs...
   like marijuana,
   heroin,
   cocaine,
   and crack.

All of these things harm the body,
and sometimes cause damage
that can't be repaired.

Drugs That Hurt the Body

Tobacco (cigarettes, cigars, smokeless tobacco)
    hurts heart and lungs
    can cause cancer and heart disease

Alcohol (beer, wine, liquor)
    destroys brain cells
    affects memory and balance
    damages brain, heart, and liver

Marijuana
    affects brain
    reduces memory and coordination
    hurts ability to learn
    damages heart and lungs

Heroin
    affects heart and lungs
    can cause difficult breathing,
      convulsions, and death
    when injected with needles, danger
      of spreading AIDS and hepatitis

Cocaine
    affects heart, breathing, body temperature
    interferes with brain's control
      of lungs and heart

Crack
    causes sleeplessness, anxiety
    damages nasal passages and lungs
    causes death

And worst of all, sometimes the body
gets used to drugs.
Then it thinks it can't
get along without them,
and wants more and more.

When that happens, the person inside
is no longer in charge.
The body is the master,
and the person is its slave.

That's called *dependency*.
And that's not for me!

I want to be in charge of my body,
not its slave.
I can make choices.

And I say
no to tobacco,
no to alcohol,
no to marijuana,
no to DRUGS!
Because . . .

My body is where I live...

and I can't live without it!